Leader's Guide
for group study of

By Warren W. Wiersbe

Leader's Guide prepared by
JAMES ECKHARDT
Visual aids by
JOE RAGONT

Instructions and 14 transparency masters (or visuals) included in a removable center section.

Seventh printing, 1982

VICTOR BOOKS

a division of SP Publications, Inc.
WHEATON, ILLINOIS 60187

Offices also in Fullerton, California • Whitby, Ontario, Canada • Amersham-on-the-Hill, Bucks, England

Suggested Teaching Methods

Brainstorming. Announce the question or topic to be "stormed." Members make as many informal suggestions as possible, not waiting to be called on. No criticism of suggestions is allowed. List suggestions on board; when all are in, have class evaluate and discuss the ideas. This method loosens up the group, involves nonparticipants, and produces new ideas.

Buzz Groups. Divide the class into groups, with from three to six persons, depending on size of class, in a group. Appoint a leader for each group or let groups select own leaders. Assign a topic to each group. Several—or all—groups can discuss same topic if necessary. Allow 5-8 minutes for discussion in the groups, then reconvene entire class and get reports from group leaders. Jot findings on board for discussion by entire class. Many persons are freer to express themselves in small groups, so this method provides maximum participation and interaction.

Discussion. Not to be confused with *Question and Answer.* In discussion, members react not only with the teacher but with one another. Usually discussion is started by the teacher asking a question to which there is more than a single acceptable answer. ("Where was the Sea of Galilee?" is hardly a discussion question!) A student will respond to a question, someone else may disagree with him, and a third person may have additional comments. The teacher is responsible for starting the discussion, keeping it "on track" by asking leading questions as necessary, and summarizing it after contributions cease. If a discussion gets out of hand and rambles, much of its value is lost.

Group (or Class) Bible Study. Each person should have his Bible open. Ask questions that will help the class learn what the passage you are studying says. Encourage sharing of insights as group discusses the interpretation of the passage and its application to current needs. Always summarize findings. This method makes students think; it shows them how to study the Bible on their own; and it increases participation and involvement.

Interview. Ask questions—or have someone in the class ask questions—of the person being interviewed. He will ordinarily be a "resource" person—one who has a fund of specialized knowledge on which you will draw. Or, an interview can be a variation on *Role Play* (see page 3).

Lecture. Needs no definition! If you lecture, aim to be *interesting*—well-prepared, enthusiastic, cordial, relevant, and with perhaps a touch of humor when it is in good taste.

Listening Groups. Same as *Buzz Groups,* except that each group is assigned a topic to listen for as someone reads a selection—Scripture or something else—or discusses a subject. When the class is reassembled as a whole, group leaders report and then the entire class evaluates the reports.

Neighbor Nudging. Like *Buzz Groups,* except that there are only two people, sitting next to each other, in each "group." In couples' classes the neighbors can be man-and-wife teams, or you may want to have the men on one set of teams and the women on another. (If a person is left out in the pairing off, assign him to one of the twosomes.) This method makes it easy for bashful persons to participate. However, since there are no group leaders, it may be hard to get some "neighbors" to speak up in the general session following the nudging.

Question and Answer. Teacher asks questions and students answer them. Makes for good interaction between teacher and students. Teacher should word questions carefully in advance—imprecise, confusing questions will be the death of this method, which provides involvement, guides group thinking, and keeps the class on the assigned topic, preventing "wandering."

Reading Groups. Same as *Buzz Groups or Listening Groups,* except that members of the group are assigned a passage of Scripture (or something else) to read and are given questions to be answered on the basis of the selection. The entire class then discusses the reports of the groups. In *Reading Groups* there are ordinarily no leaders, though in larger groups they may be helpful.

Skit. Have members read the parts of a brief script that highlights a point, provokes discussion, or presents information. Provides good variety.

Role Play. Two (or more) class members, without advance notice or written scripts, act out a situation or relationship. Give them directions as to the kind of people they are to represent and the situation in which they find themselves. They speak extemporaneously. Follow with analysis and evaluation by the class. This method helps people "feel" situations, gives them opportunity to try different solutions, and creates interest at the beginning of class. Helps apply Scripture to interpersonal relationships.

Study Groups. Like *Buzz Groups,* but instead of discussing a subject, the groups study a passage, examining it for what it says, what it means, or how it may best be applied. Each group has a leader.

Discussion is by far the best single method. If your group participates well in discussion, you will have little need for the other methods—which, after all, are designed primarily to stimulate discussion. If your class sits glumly silent instead of getting into a discussion, use other methods indicated to loosen them up.

Here are a few rules for leading discussion:
1. Maintain a relaxed, informal atmosphere.
2. Don't call on people by name to participate unless you are quite sure they are willing to do so.
3. Give a person lots of time to answer a question. If necessary, restate the question casually and informally.
4. Acknowledge any contribution, regardless of its merit.
5. Don't correct or otherwise embarrass a person who gives a wrong answer. Thank him; then ask the class, "What do the rest of you think?" or, "Has someone else another view?"
6. If some individual monopolizes the discussion, say, "On the next question, let's hear from someone who hasn't spoken yet." If necessary, ask the "monopolizer" privately, after class, to give other people more time to answer questions.
7. If someone goes off on a tangent, wait for him to draw a breath; then say, "Thanks for those interesting comments, Joe. Now let's get back to . . ." and mention the subject under consideration, or ask or restate a question that will bring the discussion back on target.
8. If someone asks a question, allow others in the group to give their answers before you give yours.

General Preparation

Survey the entire *Text* and this *Leader's Guide*. *This is basic.* Underline important passages in the text and make notes as ideas come to you, before you forget them. Become familiar with the entire course, including all units in the *Guide* that you will be using in your study. A general knowledge of what is coming up later will enable you to conduct each session more effectively and to keep discussion relevant to the subject at hand. If questions are asked that will be considered later in the course, postpone discussion until that time.

Add to your teaching notes any material and ideas you think important or of special help to your class. As teacher, your enthusiasm for the subject and your personal interest in those you teach, will in large measure determine the interest and response of your class.

We recommend strongly that you plan to use teaching aids, even if you merely jot down a word or two on a chalkboard from time to time to impress a point on the class. When you ask for a number of answers to a question, as in brainstorming, always jot down each answer in capsule form, to keep all ideas before the group. If no chalkboard is available, use a magic marker on large sheets of newsprint over a suitable easel. A printer can supply such paper for you at modest cost.

Once you have decided what visual or audio aids you will use, make sure *all* the necessary equipment is on hand *before* classtime. If you use electrical equipment such as projector or recorder, make sure you have an extension cord available if needed. For chalkboards, have chalk and eraser. That's obvious, of course, but small details are easily forgotten.

Encourage class members to bring Bibles or New Testaments to class and use them. It is good to have several modern-speech translations on hand for purposes of comparison.

Getting Started Right

Start on time. This is especially important for the first session for two reasons. First, it will set the pattern for the rest of the course. If you begin the first lesson late, members will have less reason for being on time at the others. Those who are punctual will be robbed of time, and those who are habitually late will come still later next time. Second, the first session should begin promptly because getting acquainted, explaining the procedure, and introducing the textbook will shorten your study time as it is.

Begin with prayer, asking the Holy Spirit to open hearts and minds, to give understanding, and to apply the truths that are studied. The Holy Spirit is the great Teacher. No teaching, however orthodox and carefully presented, can be truly Christian or spiritual without His control.

Involve everyone. The suggested plans for each session provide a maximum of participation for members of your class. This is important because—

1. People are usually more interested if they take part.
2. People remember more of what they discuss together than they

4

do of what they are told by a lecturer.

3. People like to help arrive at conclusions and applications. They are more likely to act on truth if they apply it to themselves than if it is applied to them by someone else.

To promote relaxed involvement, you may find it wise to—

1. Have the class sit in a circle or semicircle. Some who are not used to this idea may feel uncomfortable at first, but the arrangement makes class members feel more at home. It will also make discussion easier and more relaxed.
2. Remain seated while you teach (unless the class numbers over 25).
3. Be relaxed in your own attitude and manner. Remember that the class is not "yours," but the Lord's, so don't get tense!
4. Use some means to get the class better acquainted, unless all are well-known to each other. At the first meeting or two each member could wear a large-lettered name tag. Each one might also briefly tell something about himself, and perhaps tell what, specifically, he expects to get from this study.

Adapting the Course

This material is designed for quarterly use on a weekly basis, but it may be readily adapted to different uses. Those who wish to teach the course over a 12- or 13-week period may simply follow the lesson arrangement as it is given in this *Guide,* using or excluding review/examination sessions as desired.

For 10 sessions, the class may combine four of the shorter lessons into two. The same procedure should be followed for five sessions. However, if the material is to be covered in five sessions, each one should be two hours long with a 10-minute break near the middle. Divide the text chapters among the sessions as needed.

An Alternate Approach

The lesson plans outlined for each session in this *Guide* assume that class members are reading their texts before each class meets. The teacher should make every effort to spark interest in the text by giving members provocative assignments (as suggested under each session) and by such methods as reading aloud an especially fascinating passage (very brief) from the next week's text.

When for any reason, most of the class members will *not* have read the text in advance, (as when the class meets each evening in Vacation Bible School and members work during the day, or as in the first session, when texts may not have been available previously), a slightly different procedure must be followed.

At the beginning of the period, divide the class into small study groups of from four to six persons. Don't separate couples. It is not necessary for the same individuals to be grouped together each time the class meets— though if members prefer this, by all means allow them to meet together regularly.

As teacher of the class, lead one of the study groups yourself. Appoint a leader for each of the other groups. If people are reluctant to be leaders, explain that they need not teach and that they need no advance knowledge of the subject.

Allow the groups and their leaders as much as half an hour to study the textbook together. Then reassemble the class. Ask leaders to report findings or questions of unusual interest or that provoked disagreement. Ask the class the questions you want discussed, and allow questions from your students. Be sure to summarize, in closing, what has been studied. Finally, urge each member of the class to make some specific application of the lesson to his life. Use any of the material in this *Guide* that is appropriate and for which you have time.

Introduction to This Study

This *Leader's Guide* utilizes an exciting new feature—Victor Multi-use Transparency Masters in a removable center section. Depending on your own need, you may use the Victor Multi-use Transparency Masters in at least four ways.

1. Make overhead projector transparencies and add a new dimension to your teaching (it's easier than most people think—see *Instructions* in the center fold tear-out section, pp. a, b, c, d).

2. Make Ditto masters in order to run off Ditto copies for your class (see *Instructions*).

3. Use the Transparency Masters as visuals with a smaller class.

4. Use them as chalkboard illustrations or copy them on a flip chart.

In addition to the Transparency Masters, you will find regular chalkboards to use in connection with the sessions. Thus, this guide gives you many visuals to help you teach this vital course.

For best use of the transparencies, make a "cover sheet" out of 8½" x 11" paper, cutting out the space needed to show just part of the illustration. (See specific instructions for each MTM on page d.) Then as you teach the lesson, you will have exposed on the overhead only that part of the illustration that you are discussing. As you move through the session, you will expose or reveal the next part or parts and discuss that portion of the illustration. Having too much on the chalkboard or screen at first tends to confuse and overwhelm the student.

Bad News About the Good

News | Text, Chapter 1

Session Goals

1. To help group members get acquainted with one another.
2. To introduce the subject of Galatians (the dangers of legalism) and the background of the letter.
3. To help members grasp the author's aim in writing *Be Free:* that we will "appreciate and experience the liberty we have in Christ."

Preparation

Read the Book of Galatians in one sitting; then read it again in a reliable modern-speech translation. Study the outline of Galatians (*Text,* p. 23) and observe the structure of the letter. Then read Galatians once more with this structure in mind. Get a good grasp of the flow of Paul's argument before you begin to study the details of chapter 1.

Read chapter 1 of the text carefully. Locate the cities of Galatia on a good Bible map. Take a large map of Paul's journeys to class so you can show your students where these cities were. Read about Paul's ministry in Galatia (Acts13—14) and the founding of these churches. Take pencils and paper to class for your members to use in this first session.

Presentation

Begin this first session with a word-association game. Distribute paper and pencils to the members and ask them to write down the first thing that comes to mind when you read each of the following words: religion, law, grace, legalism, liberty, Christ, love. Now go back over the list and ask for several volunteers to tell you what they wrote down as you call out each word. Point out that these are key terms in Paul's letter to the Galatians. Law, legalism, and our liberty in Christ are recurring themes running throughout the letter.

On a large map of Paul's journeys identify the Galatian cities (Antioch in Pisidia, Iconium, Lystra, and Derbe). Trace Paul's travels as recorded in Acts 13—14 and recount his experiences in Galatia. Ask for a volunteer to read Acts 14:8-20 aloud. Ask, *What does this tell us about the temperament of the Galatians?* (They were highly emotional and changeable.) *What were the Galatian Christians now doing (Gal. 1:6-7) that caused Paul to write this letter?* (They were changing their minds again and deserting the Gospel of the grace of God.)

Use the transparency (MTM-1) on the overhead projector (or use MTM-1 as a poster) to introduce the first section of Galatians (1:1-10).

Ask someone to read these verses aloud. Point out the three parts (MTM-1) —of this section and ask your members which verses go with each part. Ask, *Why do you think Paul omitted the thanksgiving with which he opened most of his letters?* (He was not thankful for their actions and wanted to get right to the heart of the matter.)

How had Paul become an apostle (v. 1)? *Why, in terms of the Galatian situation, was that important?* (*Text,* p. 13). *What two central facts of the Gospel are set forth in verses 1 and 4?* (Christ's death and resurrection; see 1 Cor. 15:3-5.) *How were the false teachers (Judaizers) perverting the Gospel?* (*Text,* pp. 15-18)

Ask, *What is legalism?* (Refer to the earlier word associations and recall some of the words members wrote down in response to legalism.) Dr. Charles Ryrie defines legalism (display MTM-13) as "that fleshly attitude which conforms to a code in order to glorify self. It is not the code itself. Neither is it participation or non-participation. It is the *attitude* with which we approach the standards of the code and ultimately the God who authored it" (*The Grace of God,* p. 120). Legalism then is the view that we can please God or improve our standing with Him by our own efforts.

Notice the "so soon" ("so quickly," NASB) in verse 6. *How does this fit in with what we know of the Galatian temperament?* (see Acts 14:8-20) *Do you see any danger in a quick change of mind? Even in becoming a Christian? Why or why not?* (Yes, because we may make a snap decision based on insufficient evidence and then turn away from it later. A decision too easily reached may be easily reversed. The Jews at Berea [Acts 17:11-12] were commended not only because they believed the Gospel, but because they took time to check it against the Scriptures before believing it.)

Modern religious cults are perversions of the Gospel in that they often include "Jesus" plus other things in their scheme of "salvation." *What are some of these other things?* (chalkboard 1) *What is the danger in doing this?* ("You cannot mix grace and works," *Text,* p. 16.)

Dr. Wiersbe points out (*Text,* p. 16) that "the Christian life is a living relationship with God through Jesus Christ." If you have unsaved members in your group, be sure they understand this fact. It doesn't hurt to remind Christians of it either.

CHRISTIANITY IS CHRIST (Matt. 17:5, 8)
CULTS ARE "JESUS" PLUS
—works
—ritual
—knowledge
—membership
—rule keeping
—etc.

Chalkboard 1
As you discuss modern perversions of the Gospel, remind your group that the disciples on the Mount of Transfiguration were told that Jesus Christ is all they need—He is sufficient (Matt. 17:1-8). Many cults claim to accept Jesus, but add their own teachings as well. This perverts and destroys the Gospel of the grace of God.

How does a Christian differ from a legalist? (The legalist depends on his own power, resources, abilities, etc. while the Christian is to depend on God's power, direction, etc. Use MTM-14 to visualize the contrasts.) Paul's answer to the problem of legalism is developed in this letter. Take a few minutes to give an overview of the letter so your members will see where they're going in the course of this study. The outline (*Text,* p. 23) is like a road map; it lays the whole letter out before you so you can see each part in relation to the whole.

As you conclude this session, focus attention once again on the simple Gospel message. The Gospel is mentioned four times in the first ten verses of Galatians. It is important that we know it, believe it, and be able to share it with others. Distribute paper and pencils and ask each member to write out in a short paragraph the basic facts of the Gospel and how a person becomes a Christian. Then ask for two or three volunteers to share their answers with the group. You may want to summarize by using chalkboard 2. Encourage any who may be unsaved or unsure of their salvation to talk with you about it after the session is over.

Assignment

If the textbooks were distributed during this session, your members will want to read chapter 1 as well as chapter 2 for next week—and remind them to read the author's brief introduction. At any rate you will want them to read Galatians 1 several times during the week, and, if possible, to read the entire book through at one sitting. Encourage them to refer to the outline (*Text,* p. 23) as they read Galatians. Assign the two reports you will need for the next session and offer to help those preparing them if they need your assistance during the week.

This guide contains material for 12 sessions corresponding with the 12 chapters in the text. A brief review is incorporated with session 12. If you have 13 weeks of study, you can devote a separate week for review or divide one of the longer sessions (such as this one or session 10) over two weeks.

Chalkboard 2
Use this sketch to summarize the message of the Gospel as it is set forth in the opening verses of Galatians.

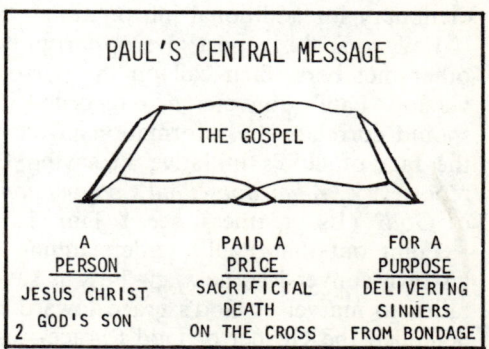

PAUL'S CENTRAL MESSAGE

THE GOSPEL

A PERSON	PAID A PRICE	FOR A PURPOSE
JESUS CHRIST GOD'S SON	SACRIFICIAL DEATH ON THE CROSS	DELIVERING SINNERS FROM BONDAGE

2

Born Free! | *Text, Chapter 2*

Session Goals
1. To discover how Paul viewed his conversion and early ministry.
2. To appreciate the greatness of God's grace and power in transforming Paul's life.

Preparation
Study chapter 2 in the textbook as you reread Galatians 1. You will find it helpful to reread the entire book of Galatians *each week* as you prepare these lessons. Saturate your mind and heart with its teachings. During the week, check with those who are preparing reports on Paul's background in Judaism and on his conversion. Offer any assistance they may need in preparing these reports.

Presentation
Begin where you left off last session, talking about the Gospel. You may want to have chalkboard 2 on the board as you do so. Ask, *What is the origin (Gal. 1:11-12) of the Gospel Paul preached?* (He received it from Christ by revelation.) *Why was that important for Paul to mention in this letter?* (Paul was stressing his independence from the Jerusalem apostles —to whom the Judaizers likely appealed for support—for his authority came directly from Christ.)

Paul's background and training in Judaism played an important part in shaping his life and thinking. Call on the assigned person to report on Paul's background, training, and activities in Judaism. The following passages will be helpful to him in preparing his report: Galatians 1:13-14; Philippians 3:4-6; Acts 8:1, 3; 9:1, 13-14; 22:3-5; 26:9-11, 24; 1 Corinthians 15:9; and 1 Timothy 1:13. He may also want to consult a Bible dictionary for additional information.

Following this report give opportunity for comments or questions from other members; then call on the person who will report on Paul's conversion. Paul's conversion is recorded in Acts 9, 22, and 26. The report should correlate the information given in these three passages and stress the fact of God's initiative in saving Paul (Gal. 1:15). Following this report, ask, *What does Paul's conversion teach about the grace and power of God?* (Its greatness; see 1 Tim. 1:12-16.)

Point out that Paul's understanding of the Gospel was influenced by his own conversion; he *knew* he was saved by the *grace* of God. He never failed to marvel at God's grace toward him and continually preached and defended the Gospel of God's grace—as in writing to the Galatians. Use chalkboard 3 to explain the theology of Paul's conversion as he understood it (*Text,* pp. 28-30).

In response to God's grace, what ought to be the motivation for Christian life and service? (To answer this question, have various members find and read the following verses: Rom. 11:36; 16:27; Eph. 1:6; 3:20-21; Phil. 4:20; 1 Cor. 10:31. We should do everything to the glory of God.) Contrast this with what Paul says is the motivation of the Judaizers (Gal. 6:11-18).

Why do you think God kept Paul separated from the apostles in Jerusalem? (*Text,* p. 32) Review, with a map, Paul's travels following his conversion: Arabia (Gal. 1:17b), Damascus (1:17c), Jerusalem (1:18-20; Acts 9:26-28), and Tarsus (Gal. 1:21-23; Acts 9:28-30).

Display MTM-2 which summarizes the biographical information Paul gives in this section (1:11-24) of Galatians. Ask, *Why do you think Paul included this biographical information in his letter?* ("Paul's argument is conclusive: his past conduct as a persecutor of the church plus the dramatic change that he experienced prove that his message and ministry are from God," *Text,* p. 28. Paul certified his background in Judaism—legalism, law-keeping, etc.—and says that since God saved him out of it, why should he—or they—want to reenter it?)

Paul's life is a testimony to the transforming power of God's grace through the Gospel. *What effect does your personal testimony have on those who know of your conversion to Christ? How many people know of your conversion?* (This is a rhetorical question, but should cause members to realize the positive—or negative—influence their lives can have on unbelievers as well as on other Christians. Our lives should reflect the truth of the Gospel and be to the glory of God.) Close in prayer thanking God for His grace at work in your lives.

Assignment

Read chapter 3 in the textbook and study Galatians 2. Assign the character sketch reports needed for the next session. These should be brief, no more than one or two minutes each.

Chalkboard 3
Paul's theology was shaped by his conversion experience as well as by revelation from Christ. Here is Paul's statement of the Gospel as he experienced it in his own life.

PAUL'S SALVATION	
GOD DID IT	(Gal. 1:15a)
☑ BY GRACE	(1:15b)
☑ THROUGH CHRIST	(1:16a)
☑ FOR OTHERS	(1:16b)
☑ FOR HIS GLORY	(1:24)

3

The Freedom Fighter, Part I / Text, Chapter 3

Session Goals

1. To see how Galatians 2:1-10 correlates with the events recorded in Acts 15:1-35.
2. To understand the nature of the problem the Judaizers represented.
3. To discover biblical principles for resolving differences within the church.

Preparation

Study chapter 3 in the textbook. Read Galatians 2 and study the events recorded in verses 1-10 in connection with Acts 15. Be sure you understand the order of events at the Jerusalem conference. Check with those who are preparing character sketches to be sure they will have them to report in this session.

Presentation

Point out that the whole book of Galatians is a defense of the Gospel of the grace of God. This was not the first time, however, that Paul defended the Gospel. He had defended it in person in a conference of church leaders in Jerusalem about A.D. 50. Galatians 2:1-10 and Acts 15 record this conference.

Ask, *What (Gal. 2:1; Acts 15:1-2) caused Paul to make this trip to Jerusalem?* (Judaizers were teaching that Gentiles had to accept the Jewish rite of circumcision and keep the Law of Moses before they could be saved. *Text*, p. 40.)

Describe (using MTM-3) the events of the meetings in Jerusalem. Acts 15 records the public convocation and the decisions reached by the council. Before going further, call on the members who have prepared character sketches on the main participants in the conference. Paul's biography was studied last session, but a number of others played a part in the decision: Barnabas, Titus, Peter, John, and James all deserve special attention. (Information for these reports can be obtained from a Bible dictionary or by looking up references to these men in a Bible concordance and seeing what the Scriptures record about each one. The reports should be brief, no more than one or two minutes each.)

What do you think the Judaizers were trying to accomplish? (To divide and conquer by causing internal dissension; or to keep the church within the Jewish fold and under the control of Judaism—as another sect of Judaism, like the Pharisees, Sadducees, and Essenes.)

Identify the various points of view (chalkboard 4) represented in the

12

conference. *What role did Titus play in the council's decision? (Text,* p. 42) *What was Paul's policy (Gal. 2:5) in dealing with the Judaizers?* (Don't give an inch!) Consider these factors which contributed to the decision reached by the council:

1. Paul and Barnabas met privately with the apostles to present their case to them before the public meeting (Gal. 2:2).

2. God had changed Peter's attitude by bringing him to Cornelius and showing him that Gentiles could be saved apart from Judaism (Acts 10—11).

3. Barnabas is mentioned ahead of Paul (Acts 15:12) and apparently took the lead in presenting their case. He was widely respected by the Jewish Chrstians; Paul was still suspect (see Acts 21:20-21).

4. James, a staunch Jewish Christian, supported Gentile salvation from the Old Testament (Acts 15:13-18).

5. Apparently all points of view (see chalkboard 4) were allowed to be expressed before the decision was announced.

Ask, *How did these factors contribute to the right decision and at the same time maintain the unity of the church?* (Opinion question, but advance preparation, opportunity for all to be heard, and adherence to the Scriptures all contributed.)

Note the two decisions of the council: (1) that Jews and Gentiles are saved the same way—through faith in Christ (Acts 15:19; Gal. 2:3-5), and (2) that Christians need to show loving concern for others by helping the poor (Gal. 2:10) and by limiting their personal freedom so as not to needlessly offend unbelieving Jews (Acts 15:20-21). *What division of responsibility (Gal. 2:7) was decided upon? (Text,* pp. 44-45)

Ask, *Before you became a Christian, what did you think you had to do to become acceptable to God?* (Opinion question, but see list of works in *Text,* p. 44.) Use chalkboard 5 to illustrate the difference between the

Chalkboard 4
Some see evidence of five points of view in the Jerusalem Council. On the one hand were the Judaizers who taught that it was necessary for Gentile believers to become Jewish proselytes. Sharing a similar view were some genuinely converted Pharisees. At the other end of the theological spectrum were Paul and Barnabas, who contended for salvation by grace through faith for all people.

The unity of the Spirit was maintained within the church with the

1	SPEAKERS	4
JUDAIZERS *(false brethren)* Acts 15:1 *(Gal. 2:4)*		PAUL & BARNABAS Acts 15:12
2		3
CONVERTED PHARISEES Acts 15:5	5	PETER Acts 15:7-11
4	JAMES Acts 15:13-20	

help of Peter and James. After the converted Pharisees spoke, Peter answered from his experience with Cornelius. Paul and Barnabas testified to the effectiveness of the Gospel among the Gentiles, and James added the weight of Scripture and stated the conclusion of the council. In all of their deliberations, they were conscious of the leading of the Holy Spirit (Acts 15: 28).

true Gospel and the false gospel preached by the Judaizers.

We might assume that the Jerusalem council's decision ended the problem, but it didn't. The dispute had begun in the church in Syrian Antioch (Acts 15:1) and would flare up there again (Gal. 2:11-21) and eventually spread to the churches in Galatia. That's why Paul had to write this letter. False teaching is not easily stamped out. That's one reason we need to know the truth of God's Word so we can spot and counteract false teaching when it rears its ugly head.

Assignment

Read Galatians 2:11-21 and chapter 4 in the textbook. This describes the continuing battle Paul had with the Judaizers and how they were able to lead astray—for a brief time—even Peter and Barnabas. We should never think we're too mature spiritually to be led astray or fall into error (Gal. 6:1).

JUDAIZERS
GRACE + LAW = SALVATION
PAUL'S GOSPEL
GRACE + FAITH = SALVATION
5

Chalkboard 5
Any message that adds any form of works to faith is a false gospel.

SESSION **4**

The Freedom Fighter, Part II / *Text, Chapter 4*

Session Goals

1. To understand the nature of Peter's actions and the danger involved.
2. To appreciate Paul's courage in rebuking him.
3. To encourage believers to live "according to the truth of the Gospel" (Gal. 2:14).

Preparation

Read and study chapter 4 in the textbook to discover *why* Peter acted as he did and the nature of the problem his actions created. Then trace the spiritual logic of Paul's rebuke in Galatians 2:11-21. If you plan to use the suggested skit, give some thought as to how you will introduce and develop it. For the concluding activity, mimeograph or ditto the questions in the chart below for each member of your group.

QUESTIONS	YES	NO	NOT SURE
1. Have I been saved by the grace of God?			
2. Am I trying to mix law and grace?			
3. Am I rejoicing in the fact that I am justified by faith in Christ?			
4. Am I walking in the liberty of grace?			
5. Am I willing to defend the truth of the Gospel?			
6. Am I "walking uprightly according to the truth of the Gospel"? (Gal. 2:14)			

Presentation

Point out that the Judaizer (legalism) problem was not eliminated by the decision of the Jerusalem conference. It followed Paul and Peter back to Antioch (Gal. 2:11-21). Ask your group to help you reenact the events described in this passage. Read the verses together and ask, *Who are the individuals and groups involved?* (Paul, Barnabas, Peter, Gentile believers, Jewish believers, Jerusalem visitors.) *What did each do?* (Peter and *all* Antioch believers ate together until the Jerusalem visitors arrived. Then Peter refused to eat with Gentile believers, and the other Jewish believers, including Barnabas, followed suit. Paul rebuked Peter for his actions and explained why he was wrong.)

Ask for volunteers to take the parts of Paul, Barnabas, and Peter. Then divide the rest of the group into Jewish believers, Gentile believers, and Jerusalem visitors (2 or 3 people). Let members improvise as they reenact the simple situation of separating from the Gentiles when the Jerusalem visitors arrive. Have the person taking Paul's part read his words to Peter (2:14b-21), preferably from a reliable modern-speech translation.

Following the reenactment, ask, *Why do you think Peter acted that way?* (Fear, *Text,* pp. 50-51) *What were two bad results of this actions?* (*Text,* pp. 51-52)

Display MTM-4 as you point out that Paul risked a break with Peter by rebuking him publicly. Paul did so in order to preserve the unity of the Antioch church. *Do you think he acted wisely? Why or why not?* (Opinion question, but consider the alternatives below.) Divide your group into teams of 3 or 4 members each and ask them to consider ways in which Paul might have responded to the situation (ignore it, talk to Peter privately,

15

etc.) and the advantages or disadvantages of each. *Which do you think would have been the best response, and why?* (A public rebuke was necessary because Peter's actions affected the entire church and they all needed to know the error of his way so they would not copy it.) Let each team report its deliberations, then discuss how similar situations should be handled in the church today.

The *Text,* (pp. 52-56) gives an excellent exposition of Paul's rebuke (Gal. 2:14-21). Discuss it with your group and be sure they understand the nature of justification by *grace* through *faith* (use chalkboard 6). Allow opportunity for questions and comments from members of your group.

Ask, *How do you think Peter responded?* (*Text,* p. 56) Read Galatians 6:1. *Do you think Paul practiced what he preached?* (Opinion question, but Paul probably displayed the meekness he recommended to others.) *How does the attitude of the "rebuker" influence the response of the "rebukee"?* (It is easier to admit our error if the person rebuking us is not acting superior to us.)

Ask, *What is your response to "the truth of the Gospel"?* (2:14) Distribute the mimeographed question form and ask each member to check off the answer that best fits his response to each question. (If you don't mimeograph the questions, distribute sheets of paper and ask each member to write down his answer as you read the questions.) If some want to talk about the question—or their answers—let them do so, but don't force anyone to participate. Encourage any who answered "No" or "Not Sure" to feel free to talk with you about their answers after the session.

Assignment

Review Galatians 1 and 2; read chapter 5 in the textbook as you study Galatians 3:1-14.

```
┌─────────────────────────────┐
│         SAVED BY            │
│        SUSTAINED BY         │
│                             │
│     GRACE THROUGH FAITH     │
│                             │
│   GOD'S       FORSAKING     │
│                             │
│   RICHES      ALL           │
│                             │
│   AT          I             │
│                             │
│   CHRIST'S    TRUST         │
│                             │
│ 6 EXPENSE     HIM           │
└─────────────────────────────┘
```

Chalkboard 6
The Bible teaches that believers are saved (and sustained) by grace through faith. These acrostics will help your members realize the true nature of grace and faith.

Instructions for Victor Multiuse Transparency Masters

As mentioned in the *Introduction to This Study* (*Guide,* p. 6), this removable center section provides Victor Multiuse Transparency Masters as important helps to your teaching this course. How transparencies can be made from them will be explained and instructions will be given for the specific use of each chalkboard or visual aid.

With educators' recognition of the teaching value of visual aids—even for adults—the Victor Multiuse Transparency Masters in this guide have been designed to give you maximum teaching help. They are numbered consecutively (MTM-1, etc.) and are coded to refer to both the guide and the text page numbers to which the illustrations relate. (The abbreviation **G**, followed by a number or numbers, refers to the page numbers in the leader's guide; the abbreviation **T**, followed by a number or numbers, refers to the page numbers in the textbook being studied.)

Some of the best visual aids available today are transparencies for overhead projection. Effective, creative teachers increasingly use transparencies to enliven class sessions and to transmit vital information to the mind through the eye-gate. Many churches already have overhead projectors, and each church should consider purchasing at least one, or one for each department. Ready-to-use transparencies are available and are becoming more so in the Christian education market, but they are expensive. However, you can make your own transparencies inexpensively through the use of transparency masters such as the ones in this guide.

Mechanics

Open up each of the staples carefully and pull out the sheets of illustrations and the one sheet of instructions. Close the staples again to keep your leader's guide together. Straighten out the illustration sheets by running a finger along the crease and file flat in a regular file folder (usually 9″ x 11¾″). Leave these instructions folded for easier reference (they are labeled as pages a, b, c, and d) and file with the transparency masters.

Making Transparencies from Masters

You can make transparencies in at least four ways:

1. *Thermal copier* (an infrared heat transfer process such as 3M's Thermofax). It is probably the fastest, most convenient, and best-known method. Simply pass the master with the appropriate film on top of the master through the copying machine (at the correct setting).

2. *Electrostatic process* (such as Xerox). Because of paper feeding requirements in these machines, care must be taken to have the correct film for the proper machine. Check before using. Also, the glass must be absolutely clean or all the dirt and dust particles will be picked up. The color on the MTM will come out gray.

3. *Photo-reflex process* (sometimes called the diffusion-transfer process). A wet process involving the exposure of a sheet of negative paper, placing it in contact with a sheet of positive paper or transparency film, and sending it through a processing machine (such as produced by Kodak, Agfa-Gevaert, and GAF Corporation).

4. *Trace your own on a transparency film.* (See below.)

Don't give up if your church does not have a copying machine. You likely live within a short distance of a machine. Try your public library, a school, or a secretarial service office (Copying or Duplicating Service in your Yellow Pages). Or maybe there's a machine at your office, or at a friend's. Usually arrangements can be made, either paying for the film or bringing your own.

You must be careful to have the right film for the right machine. To do so, first determine the type of copier that is available to you or to your friends. Then purchase the correct film from a local supplier (if not available with the machine), either an office supply house or a school supply company. If neither of these is available to you, order *A Teacher's Guide to Overhead Projection* (1969, Technifax Education Division, Holyoke, Mass. 01040), which is an excellent manual describing the production and operation of transparencies and includes the company's descriptions and prices, or *The Overhead System: Production, Implementation, and Utilization* (1972, University of Texas Visual Instruction Bureau, Drawer W, University Station, Austin, Texas 78712), which includes a valuable appendix of addresses for sources of equipment and materials. *Use Your Overhead,* by Lee Green (Victor Books, 1979) is a most helpful manual on use and production of overhead materials.

An alternate use for the transparency masters in this guide is for you to trace your own transparencies from the masters. With minimum artistic ability required, you can place a sheet of film over the master (the sheet should be at least 10″ x 7″) and trace the major part of the illustration. Exactness is not necessary and stick figures (as in the chalkboards) can be traced over the printed figures; lettering can be done separately. (For best results use .005 acetate or .003 polyester either in 8½″ x 11″ sheets or in a roll that can be cut to appropriate size.)

To write on the transparencies, use a grease pencil, preferably white, or a felt-tip marking pen (see *Materials,* page c). Grease pencil is harder to erase and does not look as neat as the felt-tip pen. Take care, however, in purchasing felt-tip marking pens, for there are a number of different kinds on the market. For transparencies you must have either erasable or nonpermanent if you wish to reuse the film (these wash off with water or a damp cloth quite easily), or permanent if you want to reuse the same visual aid. You may want to make the basic image with the permanent pen and add other material as needed with the washable one.

A further advantage of tracing your own transparencies is that you can make overlays. You expose only one part of the illustration; then, as the discussion progresses you expose the rest of it in parts or sections.

Other Uses of Transparency Masters

1. *Ditto Masters.* Another use to which the transparency masters may

b

be put is making Ditto masters from which you can run off material for each member of your class. The basic process is the same as that used for overhead transparencies. The transparency master has a thermal spirit master placed over it and is then run through a thermal copier (such as a Thermofax machine). From the master as many copies as needed are then made on any Ditto or spirit machine. If a Thermofax machine is not available, then the transparency master may be traced or copied onto a Ditto master or mimeograph, run off on the respective machines, and copies distributed to the class.

2. *Visuals.* For small classes or home Bible classes, the transparency masters may be used just as they are as visual aids to the lesson. It would be helpful to tape them or glue them to a piece of cardboard (making copies of the illustration on the back) and then prop up the visual against some books or with a homemade prop behind it. You are then free to refer to it during the lecture or discussion as it stands on the table near you.

3. *Chalkboards.* You may also use the transparency masters just as you do the other chalkboards in the guide. Simply copy the illustration onto a chalkboard or flip chart and use it as needed in your presentation (see *General Preparation,* third and fourth paragraphs, *Guide,* p. 4).

The Use of Color

In all of the methods discussed above (except that of Visuals) the colors on the transparency masters are to serve as guides to the teacher in coloring his transparencies, dittos, or chalkboards. The colors will not reproduce in the various processes (except in the Xerox, where the color turns out to be a gray shading), but will serve as guides for emphasis and distinction as the teacher colors in his transparencies.

Materials

The following is a partial list of materials necessary for the maximum use of transparencies, either through a mechanical copying process or homemade.

1. *Transparency Film.* 3M Corporation makes clear transparency film for the infrared process, 100 sheets to a box. LABELON Projection Transparencies—Infrared, 100 sheets to a box (TR-85). Also available in kits, which include clear and colored acetates, pens, frames, grease pencils, and instructions.

2. *Ditto Masters.* 3M Corporation; Klean Write KEM-FAX Spirit Masters (No. 321-D); and Heyer's Thermal Spirit Masters (No. 450 Purple).

3. *Pens.* These are available in many colors, both permanent and washable (but make sure that the kind you get will write on acetate).

Permanent—Sanford's (Bellwood, Ill. 60104) Vis-à-Vis Sharpie Pens; Eberhard Faber's Projectachrome Overhead Projector Markers (permanent); and 3M Visual Products Transparency Marking Pens (permanent).

Washable—Sanford's Vis-à-Vis Visual Aid Pens; Eberhard Faber and 3M clearly marked "nonpermanent."

4. *Grease Pencils.* Widely available in any office supply store.

Victor Multi-use Transparency Masters for This Guide

The following are some brief suggestions for using the multi-use transparency masters in the leader's guide for *Be Free*. Transparency masters numbered 1 through 12 are for those respective chapters; 13 and 14 are used in a number of the sessions.

MTM-1 (*Guide,* pp. 7-8) Display as you introduce the subject of Galatians 1:1-10. Use it again as a review in session 5 (*Guide,* p. 17).

MTM-2 (*Guide,* p. 11) Display this one as you summarize Paul's pre-conversion experiences, and again as a review in session 5 (*Guide,* p. 17).

MTM-3 (*Guide,* p. 12) Display as you outline the events connected with the Jerusalem conference, and again in session 5 (*Guide,* p. 17).

MTM-4 (*Guide,* p. 15) Display before you divide into teams to discuss Paul's options, and again for review in session 5 (*Guide,* p. 17).

MTM-5 (*Guide,* p. 17) Display as you preview Paul's six arguments presented in Galatians 3—4. Use it to review these arguments in session 6 (*Guide,* p. 19), session 7, (*Guide,* p. 21), and session 8 (*Guide,* p. 23).

MTM-6 (*Guide,* p. 19) Display to show how the Law only reveals sin, but Grace cleanses from sin.

MTM-7 (*Guide,* p. 21) Display this visual as you discuss what legalism pretends to do.

MTM-8 (*Guide,* p. 23) Use this visual to introduce the allegory and again to identify the key points in it.

MTM-9 (*Guide,* p. 25) Display this one as you introduce the subject of the three reports.

MTM-10 (*Guide,* p. 27) Display this visual to show the joy of the Spirit-filled believer in contrast to the frustrated legalist.

MTM-11 (*Guide,* p. 30) Display to show how each believer carries his own burden (backpack) but how believers share heavy loads (the boat).

MTM-12 (*Guide,* p. 32) Display as you review the marks of the legalist and of Christ and to introduce the marks of Paul's suffering.

MTM-13 (*Guide,* p. 8) Use this visual to define legalism in the first session. Use it again for review in session 5 (*Guide,* p. 18) and in session 8 (*Guide,* p. 24).

MTM-14 (*Guide,* p. 9) This visual shows the difference between a believer living under law and one living under grace. Introduce this distinction in the first session. Use it for review in session 9 (*Guide,* p. 26), and again in session 12 (*Guide,* pp. 31-32).

Bewitched and Bothered | Text, Chapter 5

Session Goals
1. To understand the value of Christian experience.
2. To realize the importance of evaluating experience by Scripture.

Preparation
Review Galatians 1—2 and read chapters 3—4. Also study textbook, chapter 5. Ask several members to be prepared to share how they came to receive Christ as Saviour.

Presentation
Review briefly the biographical information Paul gives in Galatians 1—2. Display MTMs 1-4 and ask your members to recall the main points of each of the first four sections of this letter. Paul has been arguing from his own experience with the Gospel. Now (3:1-5) he reminds the Galatians of their experience in receiving Christ. Preview the six arguments Paul uses in Galatians 3—4 using MTM-5. In this session you will be looking at the first two of these arguments in more detail.

What were the Galatian believers' experiences in connection with receiving Christ? (Faith in Christ, received the Holy Spirit, suffered for Christ's sake, experienced miracles.) Our text says, "The only real evidence of conversion is the presence of the Holy Spirit in the life of the believer" (p. 65). *Do you agree or disagree? Why? Can you think of any Scripture to support or refute the statement?* (Agree because of statements in Scripture such as Rom. 8:9; 1 Cor. 6:19.)

Point out the importance of the Holy Spirit (Gal. 3:2-3) in the believer's life (chalkboard 7, *Text,* pp. 65-67). Ask, *According to our text (p. 67) believers have two spiritual parents. Who are they?* (The Spirit of God and the Word of God.)

Paul argues from experience, but argument from experience can be dangerous. *With what must it be balanced?* ("Subjective experience must be balanced with objective evidence, because experiences can change, but truth never changes" [*Text,* p. 64].) Point out that this is exactly what Paul proceeds to do in Galatians 3:6-14.

Before you turn to Paul's scriptural arguments, however, ask several members to tell how they came to receive Christ. Point out that there are many avenues *to Christ,* but that He is the only way *to God* (chalkboard 8). We, too, must test our experience by the Word of God (*Text,* p. 68). Turn now to Paul's four arguments supported by six Old Testament Scripture verses:

1. Abraham was saved by faith (Gal. 3:6-7; Gen. 15:6).
2. This salvation is for the Gentiles through faith (Gal. 3:8-9; Gen. 12:3).
3. Salvation is by grace through faith—not the law (Gal. 3:10-12; Deut. 27:26; Hab. 2:4; Lev. 18:5).
4. Salvation comes through Christ (3:13-14; Deut. 21:33).

Discuss these arguments with your group, using the helpful material you will find in the *Text*, (pp. 68-72). Be sure to emphasize the fact that the Law requires *doing* (Lev. 18:5; *Text*, p. 70). Point out the things the Law cannot do (*Text*, p. 71).

In light of all this (the inability of the Law to save or sanctify) what then is the appeal of legalism? (It "fascinates" [Gal. 3:1] and "appeals to the flesh" [Text, pp. 72-73].) Recall Ryrie's definition of legalism (*Guide*, p. 8, display MTM-13). Encourage your members to reject legalism and live to the glory of God by His grace.

Assignment

Review these first two arguments and study the logical argument which Paul presents in Galatians 3:15-39. Read about it in chapter 6 of the textbook.

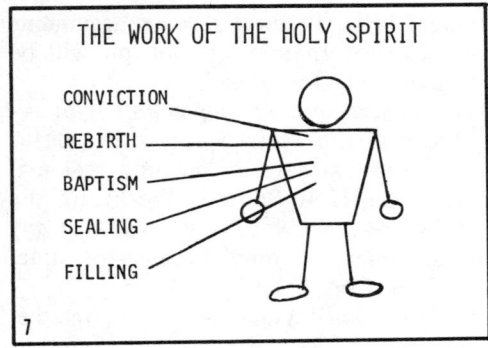

Chalkboard 7
The Law is external and unable to change a person. The Holy Spirit succeeds where the Law fails because He works inside the believer to change him into a Christlike person.

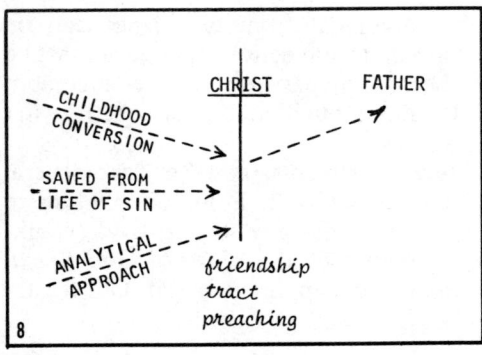

Chalkboard 8
There are many ways in which people come to Christ, but He is the only way to the Father (John 14:6). It is through faith in Christ (Gal. 3:5) that a person receives all the blessings God has for him.

The Logic of Law | Text, Chapter 6

Session Goals
1. To understand the nature and purpose of the Law.
2. To see clearly the superiority of God's promise over the Law.

Preparation
Review in your own mind the sequence of the six arguments Paul presents in Galatians 3—4. Read these chapters several times and study chapter 6 in the textbook. If you have a friend (perhaps a group member) who is a lawyer, invite him to speak to your group to explain the binding nature of contracts and wills. Ask him to bring samples to show the group. If no lawyer is available to address your group, try to get the information and samples yourself to share with the group.

Presentation
Display MTM-5 and point out that in our last session we saw that Paul quoted from the Law to prove that salvation is not by the works of the Law. The question arises: *If salvation does not involve the Law, then why was the Law given in the first place?* (*Text,* p. 75) In Galatians 3:15-29 Paul says four important things about the Law in its relationship to God's promise to Abraham. You may want to follow the four points in the text as you develop this lesson.

1. The Law cannot change the promise (3:15-18; *Text,* p. 75). Pass around samples of contracts and wills as you call on a lawyer (see *Preparation*) to explain the binding nature of such agreements. Following his explanation, ask your group, *To whom (3:15-16) did God make His promise?* (Abraham and Christ, and through Christ to all believers; *Text,* pp. 76-77.) *What two principles (3:18) are mutually exclusive?* (Law and promise.) *Can a person, then, be saved by faith plus works?* (No!)

2. The Law is not greater than the promise (3:19-20; *Text,* p. 78). *In what ways is the Law inferior to the promise?* (*Text,* pp. 78-79; chalkboard 9.) *Why were the Judaizers so impressed with the Law?* (*Text,* p. 79)

3. The Law is not contrary to the promise (3:1-26; *Text,* p. 79). Rightly understood, law and grace actually complement each other. *What was the purpose of the Law?* (*Text,* pp. 80-82) Use MTM-6 to visualize how the Law reveals sin, but only God's grace can cleanse from sin when a person trusts Christ as Saviour. Discuss the meaning of the "schoolmaster" (3:24; *Text,* pp. 81-82.)

4. The Law cannot do what the promise can do (3:27-29; *Text,* p. 83).

19

What does the grace of God do which the Law could not? (*Text*, pp. 83-85). Use chalkboard 10 to show how all the Scripture (including the Old Testament Law) speaks of Christ. Ask, *What, then, is the proper use of the Law?* (It reveals the holiness of God and the sinfulness of man.) *How could trying to obey the Law make a person willing to receive Christ?* (Failing to keep the *whole* Law perfectly, he should acknowledge his sinfulness and turn to Christ in faith for salvation [Gal. 3:24].) Encourage any unsaved members in your group to do just that as you close.

Assignment

Review Paul's three arguments in Galatians 3 and then read Galatians 4 several times, at least once in a good modern-speech translation. Study chapter 7 in the textbook. Assign the report on the biblical concept of "adoption" to be given in the next session and suggest where, in addition to the textbook, information on the subject might be found (a good Bible dictionary, for example). This is not a simple subject, so be careful to select a member who can adequately handle it.

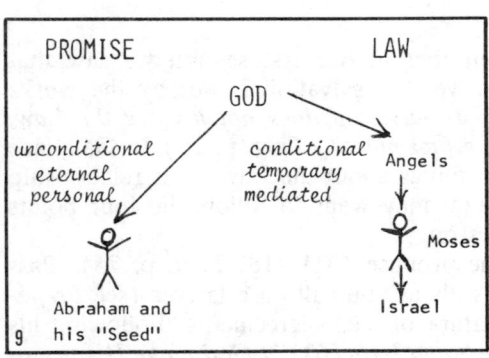

PROMISE   LAW

GOD

unconditional   *conditional* Angels
eternal   *temporary*
personal   *mediated*

                        Moses

Abraham and   Israel
9 his "Seed"

Chalkboard 9
The Law was inferior to the promise in several ways: it was conditional, temporary, and mediated (as this diagram indicates). God's promise to Abraham and his "Seed" was unconditional, eternal, and given personally.

OLD TESTAMENT	GOSPELS	ACTS— REVELATION
Preparation for Christ	*Presentation of Christ*	*Appropriation of Christ*

All by the <u>grace</u> of God!

10

Chalkboard 10
The whole of Scripture speaks of God's eternal purpose of grace in Christ. There were not two ways of salvation—by works under the Law and by faith under Grace—but salvation is by grace through faith in Christ alone (**Text**, p. 83).

It's Time to Grow Up! | Text, Chapter 7

Session Goals
1. To warn believers of the dangers of regression into legalism.
2. To understand *how* believers grow to maturity in Christ and to encourage such growth in grace.

Preparation
Review Galatians 3 and the three arguments Paul has presented so far. See where the Historical Argument (4:1-11) and the Sentimental Argument (4:12-18) fit into the total picture. Study Galatians 4:1-18 in connection with chapter 7 in the textbook. During the week, check with the person you selected to give the report on "adoption" and offer assistance if it is needed.

Presentation
Display MTM-5 and briefly review Paul's arguments up to this point. Let different members summarize the main points of each argument so far. Then display MTM-7 and point out that legalism gives the *appearance* of spiritual maturity but it actually keeps the believer in spiritual infancy. *How do legalists give the appearance of spiritual maturity?* (They set up a list of rules—often ones they find "easy" to keep—and measure themselves [and others] by their ability to keep them. They convince people that this is the way to measure spirituality.) *Why does such rule keeping (legalism) appeal to many people?* (*Text*, p. 87)

Call on the person you selected to report on the biblical concept of "adoption" (*Text*, pp. 88-89). Be sure he clearly distinguishes between regeneration and adoption and the benefits of each to the believer.

Briefly summarize Galatians 4:1-3 (*Text*, p. 89) and then ask: *What did God do for us?* (vv. 4-5) *How did He do it?* (*Text*, pp. 90-91) In writing a newspaper story the reporter gives the *who, when, where, what,* and *how*—sometimes the *why*. These are the *facts* of the story. Ask, *What facts does Paul establish in verses 4-5?* (*Text*, p. 91) Explain the meaning of "the fulness of the time" (v. 4; *Text*, p. 90). *What phrase in verse 4 refers to the Virgin Birth?* ("Made of a woman.")

Believers are God's sons (4:6-7). *How does a son differ (see 4:1-3) from a servant?* (*Text*, pp. 91-93; visualized in chalkboard 11.)

One key to understanding the nature of legalism is found in the statement: "If we observe special days like slaves, hoping to gain some spiritual merit, then we are sinning" (*Text*, p. 94). Ask, *Do you agree or disagree, and why?* Do the same with this statement: "If a man thinks

21

he is saving his soul, or *automatically* growing in grace, because of a religious observance, then he is guilty of legalism" (*Text,* p. 95).

What did Paul fear about his converts in Galatia? (v. 11) How does he next (vv. 12-18) appeal to them? (He reminds them of their earlier love for him. Notice how he balances rebuke with expressions of love.)

The text suggests (pp. 96-97) several characteristics of false teachers. What are they? Contrast this with Paul's motive in preaching the Gospel to them (*Text,* p. 96).

In contrast to the legalist's rule keeping, Paul introduces the Holy Spirit (v. 6) as the key to Christian maturity. Paul will explain the ministry of the Spirit much more fully in Galatians 5—6, but you need to mention it here so your group will see it as the alternative to legalism (see 5:18). Use chalkboard 12 as you conclude, and encourage your members to ask themselves, *Which way am I going?*

Assignment

Review Paul's arguments so far, then read Galatians 4:19-31. Point out that this is a difficult passage of Scripture and encourage them to study the explanation given in chapter 8 of the textbook carefully.

SON	SERVANT
has a father	has a master
same nature as father	different nature
obeys out of love	obeys out of fear
is rich	is poor
has a future	no future

11

Chalkboard 11
Print **son** and **servant** on the board and fill in the contrasting characteristics as your members find them (Text, pp. 91-93).

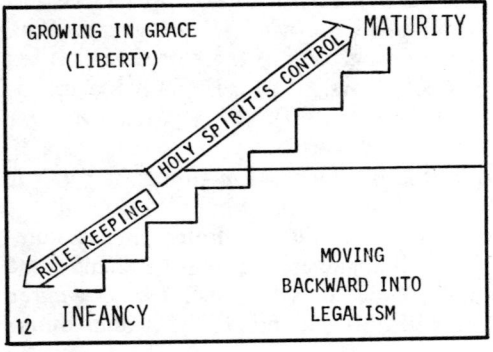

12

Chalkboard 12
Sketch this diagram on the board as you conclude the lesson by asking your members to consider: "Which way am I going?" Encourage them to yield to the Holy Spirit as God's method for growth in grace.

Meet Your Mother | Text, Chapter 8

Session Goals
1. To help believers see the spiritual bankruptcy of legalism.
2. To help believers realize, appreciate, and take advantage of their relationship to their heavenly Father.

Preparation
Galatians 4:19-31 is, for many people, an obscure passage of Scripture and may be difficult for your members to comprehend. Dr. Wiersbe's exposition of it in chapter 8 of the textbook is clear and concise and should be helpful to you and your group. You may want to stick pretty close to it in your presentation using a combination of lecture and discussion methods.

Presentation
Use MTM-5 to review Paul's arguments thus far in Galatians 3—4. Point out that in Paul's day the New Testament was just being written and that both Christians and Jews accepted the Old Testament (the Law) as God's authoritative revelation. For that reason, we find Paul using the Law (the Old Testament Scriptures) to refute legalism. Here (Gal. 4:19-31) Paul turns to the Book of Genesis to drive home his argument. He uses the account of Abraham, Sarah, Hagar, Ishmael, and Isaac as an allegory and explains its spiritual significance for the Christian. Dr. Wiersbe defines an allegory as "a narrative that has a deeper meaning behind it" (*Text,* p. 100). Be sure your members understand what an allegory is—and the danger of trying to find hidden meanings in all Old Testament events (*Text,* p. 100). Display MTM-8 as you introduce the story of Sarah and Hagar (Gen. 16; 21).

Briefly outline the key events in Abraham's life (*Text,* pp. 100-102) using chalkboard 13. These are the historical *facts* on which Paul bases his allegorical interpretation. Display MTM-8 again; it is similar to the chart on page 102 of the *Text.* Point out the interpretation Paul gives to each part of the story.

Now take a look at Isaac and the truths about salvation which he represents (*Text,* pp. 102-103; chalkboard 14). *Hagar represents the Law; in what ways was she inferior to Sarah (Grace)?* (Let members suggest and discuss the answers given in *Text,* pp. 104-107.)

How should we respond when the Law and our old nature (Hagar and Ishmael) trouble us and try to bring us into bondage? (Discuss the three options presented in *Text,* pp. 107-108.)

Dr. Wiersbe says that *"legalism* does not mean the setting of spiritual standards; it means worshiping these standards and thinking that we are spiritual because we obey them. It also means judging other believers on the basis of these standards" (*Text,* p. 108). This is a key statement and differentiates between obeying God's rules (laws) under the control of the Spirit—which is the right thing to do—and *legalism.* Be sure your members see this distinction. Display MTM-13 as you point out that legalism is the *attitude* we take toward the rules and the purpose we have in obeying them.

What is there about rules, ceremonies, and ritual that attracts people? What is the potential danger in such "forms" of religion? (*Text,* pp. 108-110) Point out that the Holy Spirit is the secret to successful Christian living and preview briefly Galatians 5—6 where the Holy Spirit is mentioned 10 times.

Assignment

Read Galatians 5—6, the final section of Paul's letter; then reread 5:1-12 and study textbook chapter 9. Assign the three reports you will need for the next session. The second (Gal. 5:2-6) is the most extensive; select a mature believer to give it.

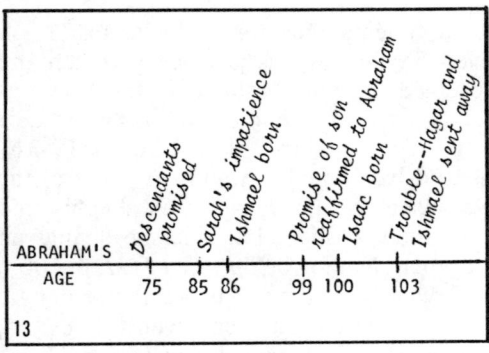

ABRAHAM'S AGE

Descendants promised — Sarah's impatience — Ishmael born — Promise of son reaffirmed to Abraham — Isaac born — Trouble--Hagar and Ishmael sent away

75   85 86   99 100   103

13

Chalkboard 13
Identify the key events of Abraham's life with Sarah and Hagar on the time-line as suggested in this diagram. This will give your members a way to visualize the facts on which Paul bases his allegorical interpretation.

ISAAC   (THE BELIEVER)

● BORN BY GOD'S POWER

● BROUGHT JOY

● GREW AND WAS WEANED

● PERSECUTED BY ISHMAEL

Hagar versus Sarah = Law versus Grace

Ishmael versus Isaac = Flesh versus Spirit

14

Chalkboard 14
Isaac represents the believer who is born of God's Spirit. List the truths Paul develops in this connection and summarize the four identifications at the bottom of the board (**Text,** pp. 102-103).

24

Stop! Thief! | *Text, Chapter 9*

Session Goals
1. To discover what a believer loses if he returns to legalism.
2. To understand the nature of true Christian liberty and its relationship to the grace of God.
3. To encourage believers to walk in liberty and grow in grace.

Preparation
Read Galatians through at least once, reviewing Paul's arguments through chapter 4. Check the outline (*Text*, p. 23) to see how chapters 5 and 6 fit into the total picture (*Text*, p. 113). Study chapter 9 in the textbook. During the week, meet in a group with the three persons who are preparing reports and go over their reports with them. Such a group study will help them better prepare their reports; it will also give you an opportunity to get better acquainted and build fellowship within your group.

Presentation
Point out that one tactic legalists have used with much success throughout the centuries is that of setting up false contrasts (*Text*, p. 113). They will tell you that the only alternative to *legalism* is *license*—total disregard for God's laws. Since license is obviously wrong, they say, the best thing to do is to accept their rules and live by them to the best of your ability. Use chalkboard 15 to show that both *legalism* and *license* are wrong—true Christian liberty is God's way.

Read Romans 8:1-4 and ask, *What is the legalist attempting to do that is impossible?* (To change, or at least control, the flesh by a set of rules.) The Holy Spirit *inside* does what no rules—however good—can do (*Text*, p. 114, chalkboard 16). Give a quick overview of Galatians 5—6 (*Text*, p. 114). Ask, *How does this compare with the spiritual "progress" of the legalist?* (*Text*, pp. 114-115)

Stress the fact that "when you abandon grace for law, *you always lose*" (*Text*, p. 115). Display MTM-9 to show what legalism robs the believer of. Introduce the reports on each of these three points that are developed in chapter 9 of the textbook:
1. The slave—you lose your liberty (Gal. 5:1; *Text*, pp. 115-116).
2. The debtor—you lose your wealth (Gal. 5:2-6; *Text*, pp. 116-120).
3. The runner—you lose your direction (Gal. 5:7-12; *Text*, pp. 120-123).

Allow time for questions and comments following each report. After all three have been given, go back and emphasize the following key points in the text.

Ask, *How does living by grace differ from living by law?* ("To live by grace means to depend on God's abundant supply for every need. To live by law means to depend on my own strength—the flesh—and be left to get by without God's supply" *Text,* p. 118; use MTM-14 to visualize the contrast.)

Many people seem to think they can please God if they keep most of the Law most of the time. *Why is this not true?* (The Law is an all-or-nothing proposition) (*Text,* pp. 118-119.) *What does it mean (Gal. 5:4) to fall from grace?* (*Text,* p. 119) Stress the fact that you can't live by law and grace at the same time. It's an either/or proposition—not both/and (*Text,* p. 119).

Many Scripture verses teach the manifold grace of God. Ask for volunteers to read the following ones aloud as you call for them; after each is read, ask, *What does this teach about the grace of God?* (A brief explanation of each is given in the *Text,* p. 123). Here are the verses: Ephesians 2:8-10; 1 Corinthians 15:9-10; 2 Corinthians 12:9; 2 Timothy 2:1; 1 Peter 5:10; Hebrews 4:16; Acts 20:32; Hebrews 10:29; and John 1:16. The Bible, indeed, has much to say about grace.

Refer to chalkboard 16 which shows that grace works inside the believer through the indwelling Holy Spirit. We'll see just what the Holy Spirit enables the believer to do as we study Galatians 5:13-26 in our next session.

Assignment

Read chapter 10 in the textbook as you study Galatians 5:13-26 to discover what the Holy Spirit does in the life of a believer.

LEGALISM or LICENSE
TRUE CHRISTIAN LIBERTY

15

Chalkboard 15
Print **legalism or license** on the board as you discuss these two options. Cross them out and then print **true Christian liberty,** which is God's way of sanctification.

NOT

BUT AN
INTERNAL
LEADING OF

EXTERNAL
LAW

THE
HOLY SPIRIT

16

Chalkboard 16
Sketch chalkboard 16 on the board to show that the Holy Spirit does what no rules can ever do. He changes and controls the believer from the inside. Refer to this again as you conclude the session and preview the work of the Holy Spirit presented in Galatians 5:13-26.

The Fifth Freedom | Text, Chapter 10

Session Goals

1. To understand and appreciate the Holy Spirit's working in our lives.
2. To encourage believers to "walk in the Spirit" (5:16, 25) and bear fruit (5:22-23).

Preparation

Dr. Wiersbe says that this paragraph (Gal. 5-13-26) is "perhaps the most crucial in the entire closing section of Galatians; for in it Paul explains three ministries of the Holy Spirit that enable the believer to enjoy liberty in Christ." Read the passage several times and study chapter 10 in the text thoroughly. Be sure you see the practical nature of this passage and help your group understand and apply its teachings.

Presentation

Remind your group of the false contrast the legalists make between *legalism* and *license* (chalkboard 15). Point out that they are *sometimes* correct in saying that liberty will degenerate into license; it does happen, sad to say. Paul warns against letting it happen in Galatians 5:13-15. *What two motives for action are suggested in these verses?* (Fleshly selfishness and love for others.) *How does God intend for believers to "fulfill" (v. 14) the Law?* (By love, which is the fruit of the Spirit.)

Use chalkboard 17 to visualize the three Persons of the Godhead at work in our salvation (*Text*, p. 126). Point out that God's work of grace reaches the *inner* man and changes the heart—the Law cannot do this.

Display MTM-10 to visualize the joy of the Spirit-filled believer in contrast to the frustrated legalist. The Spirit's presence *and control* in the believer's life is the key. The Holy Spirit enables the believer to do three important things the Law cannot do.

Divide your group into three teams; ask each team to prepare a brief written report on the ministry of the Spirit assigned to them. Let them also read and discuss the appropriate sections of the text, but encourage them to express these truths in their own words. The question to be answered in each report is: *What does the Holy Spirit enable the believer to do?* Here are the three Scripture passages: Galatians 5:13-15 (*Text,* pp. 126-128); 5:16-21, 24 (*Text,* pp. 129-133); 5:22-23, 25-26 (*Text,* pp. 133-136). Teams 2 and 3 need not get into *details* of the "works of the flesh" and the "fruit of the Spirit," but rather the general nature of each.

27

As each team reports, encourage questions and comments from others in the group. Use some or all of these questions in connection with the reports.

Report 1: *What does liberty become without love?* (*Text,* p. 127) *What "tools" does the Holy Spirit use to build us up in Christ?* (*Text,* p. 128)

Report 2: *What does Paul mean by "the flesh"?* (*Text,* p. 129) *How can a believer gain victory over the flesh?* (*Text,* p. 130)

Report 3: *How does "fruit" differ from "works"?* (*Text,* pp. 133-134) *What kinds of fruit are mentioned in the New Testament?* (*Text,* p. 134) *What is the difference between the* GIFT, GIFTS, *and* GRACES *(fruit) of the Spirit?* (*Text,* p. 134) Use chalkboard 18 to show that "all the other fruits are really an outgrowth of love" (*Text,* p. 134).

If time permits, discuss the nature of this "fruit" (*Text,* pp. 135-136) and contrast it with the "works" of the flesh (*Text,* pp. 130-132). Be sure to save time for these concluding questions: *What kind of "soil" does spiritual fruit need for maximum growth?* (*Text,* p. 136) *What is fruit good for?* (*Text,* p. 136) *For whose benefit is spiritual fruit produced?* (*Text,* p. 136)

Assignment

Read Galatians 6 and study textbook chapter 11 for next week.

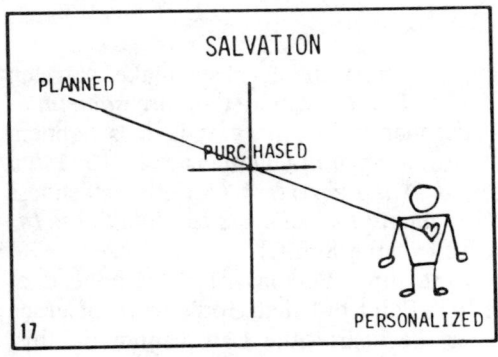

Chalkboard 17
Sketch the figures, then draw the arrow to indicate that salvation **planned** by God the Father (Eph. 1:3-6), **purchased** by God the Son (1:7-12), is **personalized** by the indwelling Holy Spirit (1:13-14).

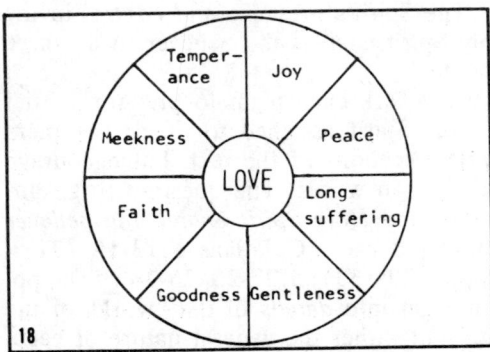

Chalkboard 18
Sketch the two circles and the spokes; print **LOVE** in large letters in the center. Then write the other fruit in the various sections as your members call them out in order. Love is the source from which all the others spring (**Text,** p. 134), and the Holy Spirit is the One who produces God's love in our hearts (Rom. 5:5).

The Liberty of Love | *Text, Chapter 11*

Session Goals
1. To discover ways in which love for others may be expressed.
2. To challenge believers to show love for one another and for all people.

Preparation
This is an extremely practical section of Paul's letter, containing a number of specific commands—some positive, some negative. Make a list of both as you study Galatians 6:1-10. Read chapter 11 in the textbook and be sure you can answer all the questions you will ask in this session. Take paper and pencils for the members of your group to use.

Presentation
Remind your group that the fruit of the Spirit (Gal. 5:22-23) is an outworking of love which the Holy Spirit produces in the heart of a yielded believer. This fruit is for the benefit of others (*Text*, p. 136). Paul is a practical man; he does not leave us with vague ideas about love, but goes on in Galatians 6:1-10 to suggest specific ways love ought to express itself. Distribute paper and pencils to your members. Ask them to read these verses and make a list of the commands—both positive and negative —they find there.

Allow several minutes for the making of these lists, then divide your members into teams of three persons each and ask each group of three to compile, from their lists, one master list of commands and then to pick out the *three* they think are most important.

Reassemble the whole group and let each team tell which three commands they selected and why. This is largely a matter of opinion with no right or wrong answers, but having to select three and then defend their selection will cause your members to seriously evaluate each command.

List the commands on the chalkboard as they are suggested. Put a check mark by those selected by more than one team. See which are selected most often. Then, if some were not selected, add these to the bottom of the list to make it complete (see chalkboard 19).

Use some or all of the following questions as you discuss these commands: *In dealing with an erring brother, how do the spiritual believer and the legalist differ as to their aim?* (*Text*, pp. 140-141) *In their attitude?* (*Text*, pp. 141-142) *How would you explain the apparent contradiction between verses 2 and 5?* (*Text*, p. 144) Display MTM-11 to illustrate the difference in the two kinds of "burdens." *What are some burdens others can help us bear? What are some we must bear ourselves?* (Opinion question, but should be in line with explanation in *Text*, p. 144.)

How does what we do with material things show the value we place on spiritual things? (*Text*, p. 145) *Give a few examples each of sowing to the flesh and of sowing to the Spirit.* (*Text*, p. 146) *What are some of the causes of spiritual fainting?* (*Text*, pp. 147-148) *To whom, and to what extent, are Christians responsible to help others?* (*Text*, p. 149)

"We share with other Christians so that all of us might be able to share with a needy world" (*Text*, p. 149). We are like radio receiver/transmitters; we receive help in order to be able to help others. Use chalkboard 20 to visualize this point. A radio transmitter reaches thousands of receivers. If each receiver were also a transmitter, think how many more receivers would be able to "pick up the signal." Each believer has *received* the Gospel and is responsible to *transmit* it to others. That's just one example of the receiver/transmitter principle. The problem in many churches is that most of the receivers are not transmitting. Ask, *What are some specific ways we can share spiritual and material blessings with others?*

POSITIVE	NEGATIVE
Restore erring brother (v. 1)	Don't think too highly of yourself (v. 3)
Bear each other's burdens (v. 2)	Don't be deceived (v. 7)
Do your own work (v. 4)	Don't sow to the flesh (v. 8)
Bear your own burden (v. 5)	Don't be weary in doing good (v. 9)
Students contribute to financial support of teachers (v. 6)	
Sow to the Spirit (v. 8)	
Do good to all people (v. 10)	
19	

Chalkboard 19
Here are the positive and negative commands in Galatians 6:1-10. List them as your teams report them—in the order they give them to you—and check off those suggested by more than one team. Some may end up with several check marks by them. Then complete the list with any your teams may not have selected.

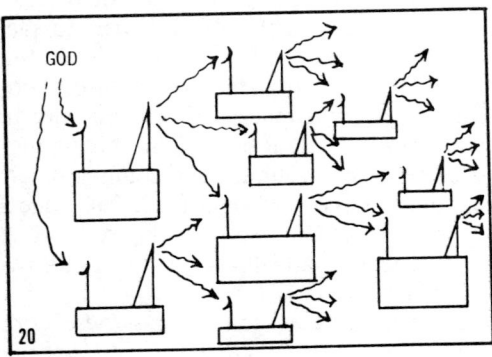

GOD

20

Chalkboard 20
Every believer is designed to be a receiver and a transmitter of the blessings (spiritual and material) of God. Each transmitter multiplies the outreach of the blessing many times over. But if some receivers are not transmitting, the blessings die there.

30

(Opinion question, but compile a list and challenge members to share more and more with others—both believers and non-believers.)

Assignment

Study Galatians 6:11-18 and read textbook chapter 12. If possible, reread the entire book of Galatians this week. Consider which section of the book has been the most help or made the greatest impression on you during this course of study. Select a favorite or key verse and be prepared to tell what it means to you.

The Marks of Freedom / Text, Chapter 12

Session Goals

1. To drive home the contrast between legalism and liberty in Christ.
2. To review the teachings of Galatians.
3. To challenge believers to allow the Holy Spirit to control their lives and help them to be and do all that Christ wants of them.

Preparation

Review the entire book of Galatians and select one or more sections that are especially meaningful to you. Also select a favorite or key verse and be prepared to tell why you chose it. Be prepared to summarize briefly—in order—Paul's arguments in favor of the Gospel of the grace of God (see outline, *Text,* p. 23). Study Galatians 6:11-18 and chapter 12 in the text. You will need paper and pencils for everyone if you ask them to write out the various ways in which they are serving Christ.

Presentation

Begin by asking, *How does the believer living under law differ from the believer living under grace?* (*Text,* p. 152) Use MTM-14 to review the contrasts between the legalist and the Spirit-filled believer. Review the *two different ways of life* described in the text (p. 152). Ask, *What is my motive for serving Christ?* (Personal question, but you may want to distribute paper and pencils and have your members list all of the things they do—in and out of church—in the service of Christ.) Then ask them to evaluate their motives for doing each. *What percentage is for praise of men, for self-esteem, to please God?* (This is not to be shared in class, so encourage them to be honest with God and themselves about their motives.)
How are the legalists described in Galatians 6:12-13? (*Text,* pp. 152-

155; write these characteristics on the board as they are given.) *What was their attitude toward the Cross? What did the cross represent to the citizen of the first century? (Text,* p. 154) *What was Paul's attitude toward the Cross of Christ, and why? (Text,* pp. 155-157) Use chalkboard 21 to illustrate the various attitudes toward the Cross found in the world of Paul's day. *Who are "the people of God" on earth today, and how did they get to be "the people of God"? (Text,* pp. 157-158)

Display MTM-12 as you review the legalist who is marked by the selfish characteristics discovered above and Christ who bears the marks of our salvation. *In what sense was Paul also a "marked man"? (Text,* p. 158) Read 2 Corinthians 11:23-28 aloud and notice the many things Paul gladly suffered for Christ's sake. Dr. Wiersbe says that "it is the Christian leader who has *suffered* for Christ who has something to offer" (*Text,* p. 159). *Do you agree or disagree? Why? Are you willing to suffer for Christ's sake in order to be a greater blessing to others? In Paul's suffering, what (2 Cor. 12:9) did he find sufficient to sustain him?* (God's grace—God sustained him, giving him the strength, courage, and ability to endure all that he did for Christ's sake. God's resources are sufficient—and they are resources of His grace.)

Notice how Paul ends his letter to the Galatians. *What key word is found in his closing sentence?* (Grace; see 1:3. His letter begins, ends, and is filled with the grace of God.) Display MTM-14 once more to contrast the two ways of life—under the law and under grace. Ask, *Which do you choose?*

Briefly review *in order* Paul's arguments for the grace of God—in salvation and in the Christian life. Refer to the outline on page 23 of the text. As time permits, encourage your members to tell you which sections of Galatians were especially meaningful or helpful to them during the course of this study. Tell which you found helpful. Then let each member tell which key verse he selected and why. Encourage unsaved members to trust Christ as Saviour and believers to walk in His grace by the power of His Holy Spirit who lives in them. Close in prayer thanking God for dealing with us in grace.

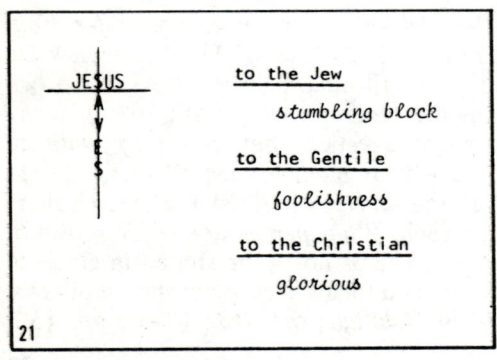

Chalkboard 21
Sketch the cross with the words **Jesus saves** on it. List the three groups on the board and write in the attitude of each to the Cross as they are discussed.

I. THE PRIVATE CONSULTATION

II. THE PUBLIC CONVOCATION

III. THE PERSONAL CONFIRMATION

RESULTS:
AL OF PAUL'S GOSPEL...
ON & AGREEMENT...UNITY

PETER GETS

A LECTURE!

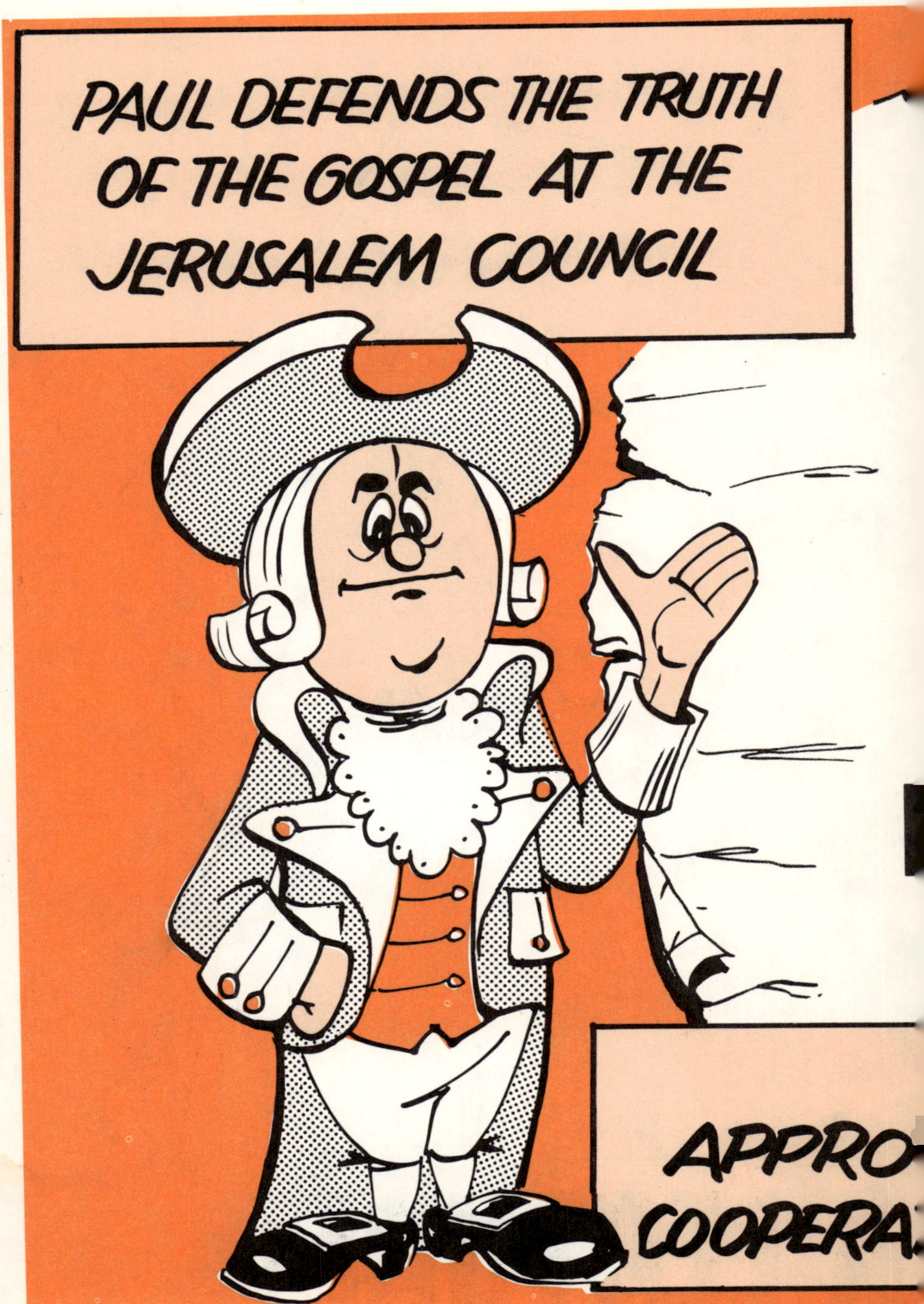

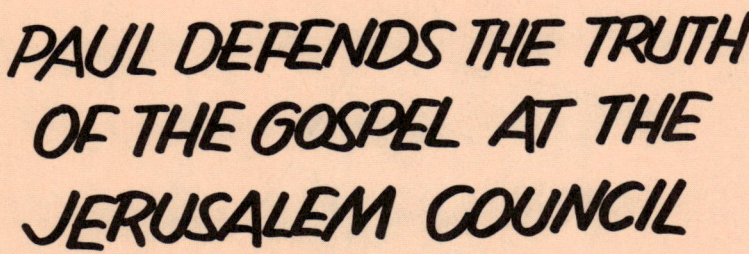

THE LAW REVEALS

GRACE CLEANSES

PAUL PRESENTS THE EVIDENCE

- PERSONAL ARGUMENT
- SCRIPTURAL ARGUMENT
- LOGICAL ARGUMENT
- HISTORICAL ARGUMENT
- SENTIMENTAL ARGUMENT
- ALLEGORICAL ARGUMENT

MTM 5

LEGALISM IS...

"THAT FLESHLY ATTITUDE WHICH CONFORMS TO A CODE IN ORDER TO GLORIFY SELF"

—CHARLES RYRIE

LAW
LIVING
I CAN DO IT MYSELF... THANK YOU!
RESULTS IN
√ PRIDE TOWARD SELF
√ CRITICAL SPIRIT TOWARD OTHERS

BY...

GRACE

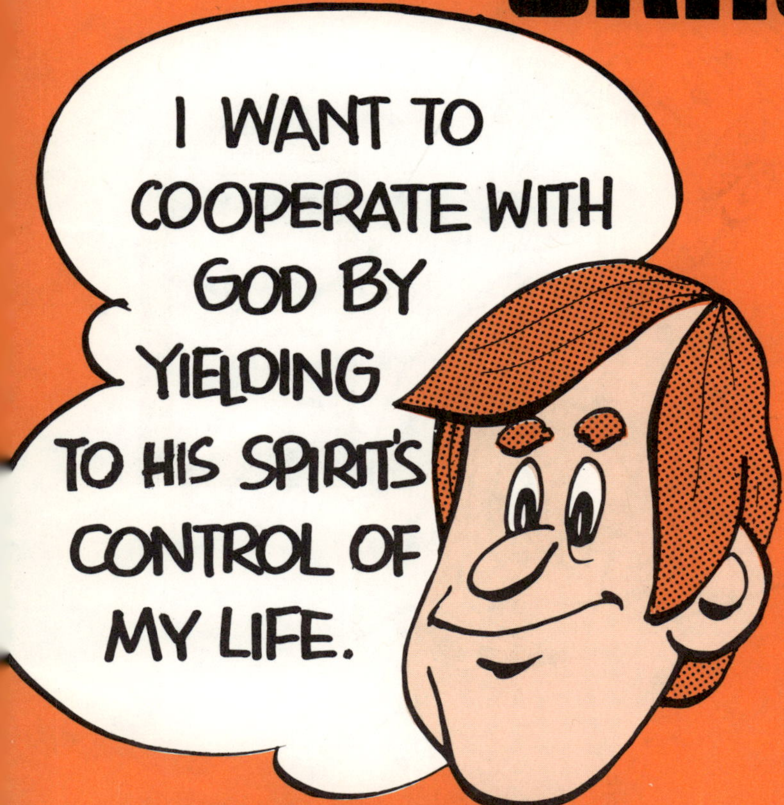

RESULTS IN

√ PRAISE TO GOD

√ CONCERN FOR OTHERS

BURDENS...

BURDENS WITH OTHERS

BRANDED!

THREE MARKED MEN

THE LEGALIST

THE LORD JESUS CHRIST

THE APOSTLE PAUL

BEARING OUR OWN

...AND SHARING

LEGALISM

ROBS THE CHRISTIAN OF HIS

√ **LIBERTY**

√ **WEALTH**

√ **DIRECTION**

SELF COMES

FILLED WITH THE HOLY SPIRIT

But inward love